FEARON'S AMAZING ADVENTURES

Y0-AGO-533

In Winter's Hand

Janice Greene

Upper Saddle River,
New Jersey

FEARON'S AMAZING ADVENTURES

Escape to Freedom
The Gringo Dies at Dawn
In Winter's Hand
The Inner Voice
Journey to the Sea
Rhino Wars
The Search
Winds of Death

Development Editor: Tony Napoli
Production Editor: Joe C. Shines
Cover Illustrator: Margaret Sanfilippo
Cover Design: Rucker Huggins

Library of Congress Catalog Card Number: 92–76010

ISBN: 0–8224–3924–7

Printed in the United States of America.

3 4 5 6 7 8 9 10 04 03 02 01 00

Contents

1

Listening to Quint

It was an awful dream. A bear was running after me, and I knew I couldn't get away. I could hear it running, close behind me. Then I woke up and opened my eyes.

Above me was the sky of Alaska, thick with stars. A foot of snow lay on the ground. Even through my bearskin blanket, I could feel the cold.

It was September already, and we were 400 miles from Nome. Our guide, Quint, told us we had to get going. He said the winter storms would begin soon. When they did, the trail to Nome would be impossible to follow.

Sonny was asleep on the other side of the dead fire. I heard him talking in his sleep, as if he were arguing with me. Sonny didn't want to start back. "Come on, Ben," he said. "We can't go back to Frisco with nothing. We'll get a break any day now! Maybe tomorrow . . ."

Sonny's tomorrows hadn't brought any luck. We'd been up here since the summer of 1897, over a year. We'd found gold, but only a little. It wasn't even enough to pay our way back to San Francisco.

Quint never has much to say. Lately, though, he's been talking to me alone. He says, "Sonny's crazy for gold. When a man gets like that, you can't trust him." I just tell Quint to shut up. I don't like him any more than Sonny does.

We can't get along without Quint, though. He's lived up here in Alaska all his life. He's the son of a French fur trader and an Aleut fisherwoman. He's taught us about hunting and sled dogs and how to pan for gold. Most important, he knows the trail to Nome.

I was just going back to sleep when something dark walked between me and the sky. I froze and listened. I heard nothing. Someone was walking through our camp without a sound.

Then I did hear something. It was a

clinking sound. Someone was getting into our bag of rifle bullets!

I reached for my rifle and fired into the air. "Who's there?" I yelled. "Speak up or I'll shoot."

I heard Sonny jump up and cock his rifle. "Ben!" he called. "Where are they?" All the dogs started barking.

"It's me!" said Quint. "Put down your guns!"

Sonny lit the lantern. There was Quint, standing next to our gear.

"What are you sneaking around for?" asked Sonny. He looked quickly through our gear. "Look!" he said to me. He showed me the sealskin bag that held our rifle bullets. It had been opened.

Sonny grabbed Quint's pack and emptied it on the snow. Out fell Quint's bearskin blanket, a package of salt, a dozen rifle bullets, and a tiny moosehide bag with some gold in it.

"You were trying to rob us!" said Sonny, grabbing Quint's jacket.

Quint quickly twisted out of his jacket. Before I could tell what he was doing, he had his knife in his hand. Its long blade was pointed at Sonny's neck.

"What do you think you're doing?" yelled Sonny. His voice was loud and nervous.

"What do you *think* I'm doing?" said Quint. His brown face looked hard as wood.

Grabbing Quint's arm, I yelled, "Stop!" I looked him in the eye. "Quint, why were you going through our gear?"

"I took my share," said Quint. "I took only enough to get to Nome."

"Ha!" said Sonny.

Quint went on, "You two don't listen to me. I say, 'Winter is coming. We must leave.' You say, 'Not yet. One more day. One more day.' You two are going to die here. Not me! I'm going back to Nome."

Sonny said, "I don't believe a word of this! He's covering up. He was going to take our gear and leave."

"He didn't have that much in his pack," I said slowly. "And he's right, Sonny. We must go now, or we'll never make it." I looked hard at him. "We must leave tomorrow."

"All right," Sonny said in a low voice. He turned to Quint and said, "If I catch you in our gear again, you're a dead man."

We went back to bed, but I was too wide awake to sleep. I thought about how we had first come to Nome. In July of 1897, news of the gold strikes in Alaska and the Yukon hit San Francisco. The papers were full of stories about gold. Sonny and I quit our jobs and took a boat to Nome.

Nome was a busy town. It never seemed to sleep. The streets were full. The bars were full. In the bars, all the talk was of gold. *Gold!* We heard of streams full of gold—so full the water shone yellow. We heard of men who got rich in a week. We also heard stories about men who lost all their gold in a night.

We listened and learned. We learned about all the gear we would need to look for gold. We bought a pick and shovel and gold pans. We bought food and blankets. We bought a sled, four dogs, and a map. We thought we'd done quite well, but we didn't have much money left. Everything cost so much in Alaska.

"You need one more thing," said an old man at a bar. "You need a guide, someone who knows the country. You can't learn all about the land from a map."

A guide seemed like a good idea, so I asked around. A couple of men told me about Quint Renaud.

The next day I met with him. "Five hundred dollars," he said, "and a third of any gold you find."

"Four hundred and a third of the gold," I said.

He nodded, and we shook hands.

Quint laughed when he saw our gear. "So much food!" he said. "You have enough to start a restaurant! And you have enough blankets for a hotel! One bearskin each is enough."

When he saw the dogs, he shook his head. Then he went up to one dog. "See that chest?" he said. "This fellow can't pull!"

He walked up to another. "Not strong! She won't last!" he told us.

None of the dogs were any good. He picked out blankets, most of the food, and some of the pots we'd bought. "Get rid of all this, and buy some good dogs," he said. "Dogs are the most important thing."

We sold a lot of our gear. Then Quint said we needed eight dogs, not four. He also said we should pay about $300 each for them. They had to be strong and healthy.

"Eight dogs! At $300 each!" said Sonny. "That's too much!"

Quint said, "If you don't get a good team, you can get yourselves another guide."

"Good idea!" said Sonny. "Come on, Ben. Let's find someone else."

"Wait a minute, Sonny," I said. "I heard about Quint from several men. He's a good guide. He just wants to be on the safe side. Isn't that right, Quint?"

Quint nodded. "If you have a bad team, you won't get back here to Nome," he said.

So we bought eight dogs and paid a lot for them. Finally we started out. Soon we learned that Quint knew what he was talking about. We learned a lot from him. He taught us how to find our way by looking at the stars, how to pan for gold, and how to follow an animal's tracks. In spite of all this, we never became friends with Quint. He was always the outsider. Sometimes when Sonny and I were talking, we even forgot Quint was there.

I closed my eyes. I wondered about the men who bought those four dogs we sold them. At last I fell asleep.

2

➤ Gold at Last!

A light snow was falling when we woke up. After breakfast, we packed the sled. The dogs knew we were getting ready to go. They barked and chased each other. Teeka, Sonny's favorite dog, kept running back and forth in front of him, barking. He laughed and threw snowballs at her. We untangled the long leather traces and laid them out on the snow. Teeka ran up to the traces, and Sonny began to fasten the leather straps on her. Kip, the lead dog, ran up to Teeka, growling.

Quint cracked his whip in the air. "No fighting!" he yelled. He turned to Sonny and said, "Kip has to get in first," he said.

"What for?" asked Sonny.

"Kip is the leader," said Quint. "He knows he's the leader. So do the other dogs." Kip stepped proudly into his traces. Then came the rest of the dogs, eight in all. At last Sonny stepped behind the sled. "Mush!" he yelled, and the dogs took off at a run. The sled moved smoothly over the snow. Quint ran ahead of the team, with me close behind him.

About noon we stopped. Quint and I lay down on the snow while Sonny led the dogs down to a stream for a drink.

He was gone a long time. As I began to wonder what was keeping him, he came running toward us, yelling something.

"What?" I called.

"Gold!" he yelled, running up to the sled. He jerked off his cap and threw it high into the air. His blond hair shook out like a lion's mane. "Gold!" he yelled. "Gold!"

Sonny led us down a hill to the stream. Below the fast-running water, I saw the shine of gold.

Sonny shoved his hand into the icy water. Out came a handful of gold! Bright flakes filled his hand and dripped from his fingers.

"I'm going to be rich," said Sonny. "I'm going to be SO RICH!" He threw back his head and laughed and laughed.

I started laughing, too. Even Quint joined in. We yelled and laughed like crazy people.

We panned for gold until dark that day, and the next day, and the next. We stopped only to eat and sleep. We bent over the stream for hours and hours. At night it hurt to stand up. We put the gold in moosehide bags, one for each of us. Every day the bags grew heavier.

Every night we'd lie around the fire, dreaming out loud about our gold. I wanted to buy a ranch. I dreamed of 100 fat cattle and a big house and barn. I also dreamed of things gold couldn't buy, such as a family. I wanted a family very much.

Sonny's dream took him back to Frisco. "I'll have the best of everything," he said, "the best money can buy. I'll walk down the streets in swell clothes." He stood up and walked around like a rooster. I started laughing. He went on, "People will whisper when I walk by. 'There goes the richest man in town,' they'll say." He laughed again.

We didn't ask Quint what he'd do with his gold. He probably wouldn't have told us anyway.

Every day, the snow fell and the weather got colder. One morning, the stream was covered with ice. Sonny kicked at it with his foot. Then he went to get the pick.

That day Sonny didn't stop to eat. When it got dark, he took the lantern down the hill to the stream and panned for gold by lantern light.

Quint and I ate dinner. Then we sat, staring at the fire. After a while, Quint said, "Sonny's gotten greedy. He'll do anything for gold now. He'll steal for it. He'll even kill for it. He's not your friend anymore."

I said what I usually say when Quint goes on about something: "Shut up."

I went down to the stream. Sonny was breaking the ice with the pick.

"Ice keeps getting in the way," he said. I watched for a minute. The ice sounded like breaking glass. Sonny's face looked ugly and strange in the lantern light.

"We're leaving tomorrow," I said.

He stopped swinging and stared at me. The sharp end of the pick shone in the light. Sonny said, "You're on Quint's side now? Is that it?"

"No," I said. "I just want to make it back

to Nome." I turned and walked back to the glowing fire.

I told Quint, "We're leaving tomorrow." Quint nodded, and I went to bed. I didn't sleep for a long time.

I thought about San Francisco and all the great times Sonny and I had had. I've always been pretty serious—*too* serious, some people say—but when I was with Sonny, I was always laughing. So many crazy nights we'd spent. There was always a crowd of people around Sonny. Men liked him, and women liked him a lot. He must know hundreds of stories. Some are true, and some he makes up as he goes along.

The best stories weren't told by Sonny, though. The best stories were those he lived. I bet people are still telling the story of Harper's Inn.

It was a cold night in February. It was warm inside the inn, though, with so many of us packed in there. Sonny had made up a game he called "Walk the Ice."

He got Harper to spread little bits of ice all over the bar. Then a man had to walk down the bar—without falling. Twelve men tried it. Sonny was the only one who didn't fall. Then this big fellow from Chicago got up on the bar. He didn't fall, either.

"We have two winners!" said Harper. "Shall we make them do it again?"

That was too easy. "Make them walk backward!" someone yelled.

"Make them walk with their eyes shut!" yelled another man.

Then Sid Clark yelled out, "The roof! Make them walk the roof!"

"That's stupid, Sid!" I said. "They'd break their necks!"

"I'll do it!" said Sonny. Everyone cheered.

"I'll have a look at the roof first," said the man from Chicago.

We all went outside. The full moon made the inn look silver. The fellow from Chicago looked at the roof. Two steep sides of the roof met in the middle. It was two stories above the ground.

The man from Chicago shook his head. "I'm not that crazy," he said.

Sonny's grin flashed in the moonlight. "Who wants to bet I'll make it across?" he shouted.

"Sonny, come on!" I said. "You don't have

to do this! If you get hurt, you'll be out of work for months!"

Sonny wasn't listening. Everyone bet, most of them betting he wouldn't make it.

There was a tree next to Harper's. Sonny climbed up the tree as far as he could. Then we threw a rope over the roof and to the tree. Sonny held onto it, and we pulled him up to the top of the roof.

Slowly, he stood up on the thin edge of the roof. Everyone cheered once more.

Then he started across. He put one foot down slowly, then the other. "Here I come!" he called. "I'm going to make it!"

His steps were slow and sure. We cheered him on. "You're going to make it!" we yelled.

Closer . . . closer . . . He made it! Everyone cheered wildly. The men got ready to throw the rope back so he could climb down. Then, Sonny turned around! He started going back!

"What are you doing?" I yelled. Sonny didn't answer. His long blond hair blew in the cold wind.

The men began to yell. Over and over again, they shouted, "Come on, Sonny! Come on, Sonny!"

He went forward by inches, closer and closer to the edge. Just three more feet and he'd be there!

All at once Sonny's foot slipped, and he fell forward. He grabbed for the edge—too late! "Ya-hoooooo!" he yelled. He slid down the roof and into the tree.

We rushed over to the tree. Sonny was hanging there upside down, laughing and laughing.

We got him down. Men were shaking his hand and patting him on the back. "I think I broke my leg," he said with a grin. We helped him back inside. Bob Skinner, the doctor's son, had a look at the leg. "It looks broken to me," he said.

I stood up on a chair. "Sonny's going to be out of work for a while," I said. "How about helping him out with a little money?"

Everyone gave something. The man from Chicago gave almost 50 dollars. Then the biggest men lifted him up and carried him off to Doc Skinner's house.

At last I closed my eyes. I fell asleep, thinking of Sonny. He had laughed and joked all the way to Doc Skinner's, broken leg and all.

3

 Heading Back

The next morning the sky was bright blue. The weather was warmer than it had been in weeks.

I pulled the dogs' traces out of the sled. "Come on, dogs!" I called. "We're really leaving this time!"

The dogs came running, every one of them barking like crazy. Suddenly, the hill behind us seemed to move. With a soft *whump*, a large piece of snow slid down and covered the dogs.

Quint laughed. "Don't worry," he said. "They'll come out."

Still barking, the dogs jumped free from the snow. As they shook themselves, bits of snow flew everywhere.

"The warm weather makes the snow slip," said Quint. "We're lucky that wasn't a big avalanche. We would have lost those dogs."

It got warmer and warmer. By noon, the snow was soft under our feet.

"I'll bet there's no ice left on that stream," said Sonny. I didn't answer.

When we stopped for the night, Sonny opened the bags of gold. "Look at that," he said softly. The shine from the gold turned his face yellow. Even his teeth were shiny yellow. He looked like an animal, almost.

"How much do you think it's worth?" he asked Quint.

"About $2,000 for each bag," said Quint. "A total of $6,000, I think."

"I thought it would be worth more," Sonny said, frowning. "We *could* go back."

"We can't," I said.

Quint said, "If you go back, you'll have to go alone."

Sonny gave us both an angry look. He turned back to the gold. "There's not enough," he said in a low voice.

"Not enough for three?" said Quint.

Sonny jumped to his feet. "I've had about enough of you! I'm sick of you!" he yelled.

Quint jumped up and faced him. His eyes were narrow with anger.

I stepped between them. "Lay off!" I said. "Both of you! Just lay off!" I turned away. "Or maybe I should just let you kill each other. Then there'd be some peace around here." I felt as though I never wanted to see either one of them again.

Sonny and I had been friends for years, but since we found gold, he was like a different person. I wasn't sure I liked him anymore.

As for Quint, Sonny and I had never liked him. He never cared for us, either. I think he liked the dogs better than he liked either Sonny or me.

The weather stayed warm. "This is bad," said Quint. "The fast way is across the Chain of Lakes. But the ice will melt if the weather doesn't get cold again."

It didn't turn cold. As we led the team through the woods, water dripped from the trees. We reached the Chain of Lakes. There were seven of them. They stretched out over 11 miles.

The first lake, called Sawtooth, was ice covered. The ice looked solid to me, but Quint frowned. He said, "I'll walk ahead." He cut himself a long branch from a tree.

"What's that for?" I asked.

"I hold it like this," said Quint. He held the branch sideways. Then he said, "If the ice breaks up, I have the pole to hang on to."

Quint walked ahead with his pole. I went next with the team, and Sonny walked right behind me. Sonny carried the gold in a pack.

We made it easily over Sawtooth Lake and the second one, Blue Cloud. We were halfway across the third lake, Tallboy, when suddenly I heard a loud cracking sound. *"Arrrgh!"* Quint yelled.

4

 **Close Calls**

A hole opened in the ice, and Quint fell in. He held on to the pole, which lay across the hole.

Sonny and I raced up to him. We grabbed the pole and pulled, and the ice began to crack under our feet. "Lie down!" Sonny yelled. "Let's try the other side!" We worked our way to the other side of the hole. Luckily the ice held.

Sonny grabbed the pole. "Pull my feet!" he said. I held his boots and pulled. Slowly, slowly, we pulled Quint onto the solid ice.

Quint's clothes were covered with ice.

"F-fire!" he said. He was shaking all over.

I ran to the sled and jerked out the bag full of wood. Quint would freeze if we didn't get him warmed up quickly.

"Matches!" I called to Sonny.

He threw them over, and I quickly got the fire going. Then I gave the matches back to Sonny. We pulled Quint's frozen clothes off him. His skin looked purple. We wrapped him up in a bearskin. He held his feet very close to the fire.

"I don't want to lose any toes," he said.

In half an hour, he was warm and dry. He drank a cup of coffee, and then he picked up his pole. "OK," he said. He started out across the ice again. Quint's really a brave man, I thought.

The shadows were long when we reached the last lake. We were starting out when Quint stopped and waved me back. "Too thin!" he called. "Too thin for the sled!"

"Whoa!" I called to the dogs. It was too late. A loud *crack!* rang in my ears. Long pieces of ice rose up, and I went under. The freezing water hit me like a hammer.

The sled was only halfway in the water, so I grabbed it and held on. Above me, the dogs were pulling as hard as they could. Their feet scratched and slipped on the ice. I heard Quint yelling, "Come on, dogs!"

I could hear the dogs panting. Very slowly, the sled moved. *Please, please hurry,*

I told them silently. I knew I couldn't hold on much longer.

Someone grabbed the hood of my jacket. "Up now, up!" Quint's voice seemed far away. Arms pulled at me, but I couldn't move to help them. I was sinking into sleep.

When they got me out, they laid me on solid ice. Quint began pulling at my boots. "The wood! Quick!" he said.

A minute later, Sonny dropped the wood in front of me. He felt his jacket pockets. A strange look came over him. He said, "The matches! They're lost!"

Quint said nothing as he pulled a flint from his pocket. He lit the fire and got dry clothes for me. Then he said, "Get up! Run around the fire." I didn't want to move, but Quint made me run until I warmed up.

"Thanks," I told Quint.

Quint nodded. "You saved me, too," he said. "You and Sonny. You might have to do it again."

We stopped there for the night. We were all too tired to go any farther. While Sonny was feeding the dogs, Quint came up to me.

"Those matches are *not* lost," he said. "I'd bet my gold. Look in Sonny's pockets."

I thought of Sonny. I remembered the way he'd looked at the gold. He'd said, "There's not enough." Quint was wrong. Sonny was my friend.

I said, "Quint, I owe you a lot. I'll never forget you saved my life. But for the last time, shut up about Sonny!"

While we ate, Sonny thanked Quint for saving my life. "You're a good man, Quint," he said. He slapped Quint lightly on the back. "Quick-thinking, too. We're lucky that you had that flint!"

Sonny said, "That was a pretty close call when you fell in, too. If it hadn't been for that pole . . ."

"Yeah," said Quint. "A pole helps."

"Anyway," Sonny said, "we had two close calls today. It's got me worried. I mean, what if we'd lost you? Ben and I wouldn't be able to get back to Nome. How about drawing us a map, just in case?"

I said, "Hey, that's a good idea."

"No," said Quint.

"Why not?" said Sonny in an angry voice.

Quint said, "If you know the trail, you don't need me. When men have gold, I make sure they really need me."

I felt like punching Quint. This afternoon, he had been the one to save my life. He'd done far more to help me than Sonny had done, but I still couldn't stand him.

We had just finished eating when a cold wind started up. It put the fire out. Snow blew across the ice. We wrapped ourselves up in our bearskins and went to sleep.

The next morning the ice looked solid everywhere, but the wind had frozen the new ice into sharp points. "This ice would cut up the dogs' feet," said Quint. "We'll make little shoes for them." He got out a piece of moosehide. He showed us how to cut it into small pieces. We tied the pieces around the dogs' feet.

"How about that," said Sonny. "Dog booties!"

"Yeah," said Quint. "We'll use them every day. They'll save the dogs' feet."

After that, we made good time. We left the lakes behind and entered the woods. The trail grew narrow. Sonny and Quint were back with the team. I walked on ahead. I was following a tight curve in the trail when suddenly I saw several red drops on the snow—blood.

5

A Stranger
in the Snow

I walked slowly around the curve. Sitting in the middle of the trail was a grizzly bear, licking its bloody foot.

The bear saw me and roared. A cold wave of fear went down my back. I aimed my rifle as the bear charged at me. Holding my breath, I pulled the trigger. The bullet went into the bear's chest, but the bear kept coming. I shot again, and the bear still didn't stop. It was right in front of me! I screamed, but no sound came out. The bear's mouth was wide open. I felt its hot, heavy breath.

Then I heard a rifle shot. The bear's head jerked to one side, and its eyes closed. It fell down on top of my legs.

A stranger ran up to me. He threw his rifle down and started rolling the bear off me. Sonny and Quint ran up and helped.

I got up slowly and rubbed my eyes. I could still see the bear's wide-open mouth in front of my face.

"Thanks," I said to the stranger.

"My name's Sam," he said. He pulled his green wool cap down to his eyebrows and stuck out his hand.

I shook it. It was small, like the rest of him. At first I thought he was about my age, 22, but then I noticed that he'd never shaved. Maybe kids grow up fast out here, I thought. "Are you out here by yourself?" I asked.

"I am now," he said. "Pa and I were on our way to Nome. This bear killed him and our four dogs, too. That was two days ago. I've been trying to get even ever since."

"You're even now," said Sonny.

"I don't know," said Sam. "Now all I've got is a dead Pa and a dead bear. Want to help me eat him?"

We did. I'd never eaten bear meat before, and it tasted fine. The kid ate as if he hadn't had a meal in a week. He asked where we were headed. When we said Nome, he asked if he could come along.

"I'm pretty good with a rifle," he said, "and I don't eat too much, usually."

"Sure," I said.

"Just a minute," said Sonny. "My partner and I have to talk about this."

We walked a little way off from the others. Sonny turned to me and said, "We can't have that kid coming along. He might find out about the gold."

"What if he does?" I said. "He saved my life back there. Maybe I'll even give him some of my gold. Besides, he can't make it back to Nome alone. He's just a kid."

"He'll do fine on his own," said Sonny. "He took care of that bear, didn't he?"

"Yes, he did," I said. "Maybe he'll save your life someday, too."

I walked back to the fire. "You can come along," I told the kid.

"Thanks," he said, but he looked worried.

The next few days, that worried look stayed with him. I tried to cheer him up, but it wasn't easy. He'd grin a little, but soon that look would come back.

Sonny and I were curious about him. We asked him where he was from. "Oregon," he said. Did he have any family besides his

Pa? "No," he said. He didn't even have a pack. How did he live in the woods without any gear? "I've got my rifle, bullets—and this," he said. He pulled a flint from his jacket pocket.

"Is that all?" I asked.

"The rest fell into Sawtooth Lake," he said. "Lucky for me, the flint didn't."

"He's hiding something," said Sonny later.

I shook my head. "I don't know," I said. "Maybe he is, but I can't figure out what." Sonny couldn't either.

Sam seemed to like Quint best. Maybe that was because Quint never asked him questions. Sam, on the other hand, asked Quint about everything: the stars, the dogs, the animals in the woods. I never knew Quint liked to talk so much.

The kid was jumpy. Once when I was cleaning my rifle, it went off. The kid dove behind a tree, his face white. Also, he never put his rifle down. When he ate, he laid it on his knees.

One afternoon, a real winter storm blew up. Everything else turned white. I couldn't tell the ground from the sky. We couldn't see eight feet ahead, so there was nothing to do but stop. I was angry with Sonny for making us start so late that we were running right into winter. I was angrier with myself for not pushing him harder.

Quint showed us how to make a shelter. We took the moosehide cover off the top of the sled. We laid it over a thick log, for a roof. Then we piled branches up on the sides. It was a small shelter, but it kept us out of the wind.

Most of the time we slept. One time Sonny started talking about all the women he'd known in San Francisco.

"Remember that time Sally and Wanda had a fight over me?" he said. "I thought they were going to pull each other's hair out." He clapped his big hands together and laughed.

I looked at the kid. He looked as if he wished he were 50 miles away. Maybe he was shy around women. After all, he was pretty young.

I said, "I'm going to get some more sleep. You might as well turn in, too, Sonny. I don't think anyone else wants to hear your stories."

Sonny looked around. Quint was asleep,

or at least his eyes were closed. Sonny
turned to Sam, who was staring at the
ground.

"You don't like me talking all the time?"
said Sonny loudly. "You want a turn? Now,
that's a good idea! Let's hear about all *your*
experiences."

"Lay off," I said. "Sam's a bit young for
that kind of talk."

"I'm tired," said the kid. He laid his rifle
next to him and curled up in his bearskin.

As I watched the kid fall asleep, for some
strange reason I started thinking about
Mary. A lot of time had gone by. It didn't
hurt to think about her anymore.

I had met Mary in San Francisco, where
she worked as a cook in a restaurant. She
was tall and pretty. Her strong hands were
always red from her work. Her voice was
beautiful.

Soon we were taking walks together every
Sunday. I fell in love with her shy smile
and beautiful voice.

I met her parents once, but they didn't
like me much. They hoped their daughter
would do better than me—a dockworker. I
let them know I wouldn't be working at the

docks forever. I didn't know what I'd be doing next, though. When I thought about it, I wanted to have a ranch. I couldn't see Mary on a ranch, though. She was a city woman. So I didn't think very far ahead. I just thought about the next Sunday, when I would see her again. We were happy together, for a while.

Often, Sonny would ask me about her. "When am I going to meet this girl of yours?" he'd say.

"Oh, sometime," I'd say. I wasn't in a hurry.

One night, I took her out for some ice cream. As we were walking down the street, we met Sonny.

"Why, you must be Mary!" he said. He took her rough, red hand as if it were glass. He bowed. His blond hair fell across his brown forehead. He said, "No wonder Ben has been keeping you a secret! You sure are pretty."

Mary looked at him with shining eyes.

After a few minutes, I said, "Well, we'd better get going. We were going to have some ice cream."

With a shy smile, Mary asked Sonny,

"Would you like to come with us?"

He certainly would. He told her jokes and stories. Mary looked at him the whole time. She looked *only* at him, in fact.

When Mary and I went out the next Sunday, she didn't say much. I tried to talk for a while, but talking with her wasn't easy anymore. As I was walking her home, she said, "Do you have to be so serious all the time? Why can't you have a laugh once in a while?"

She didn't say, "Why can't you be more like Sonny?" She might as well have.

I didn't come around the next Sunday— or ever again. I thought about her all the time, but it was no good. Sonny was the one she wanted.

Of course, in the end he didn't really want her—except for just a few weeks. I fell asleep wondering if I'd ever meet someone who liked me better than she liked Sonny.

6

◢ More Strangers

The next morning the storm had passed, and we hit the trail early. Before long, we reached Leggit Pass. Quint said that was halfway to Nome. That news made us feel pretty good. The trail seemed easy. Sam and I were walking on ahead. Quint and Sonny were behind with the team.

We were almost to the top of the pass. The trail was narrow. It was cut into the side of the mountain. All at once, Sam said, "Oh, no!"

"What?" I said. "What's wrong?"

"Up there!" he said. He grabbed my arm. "Look up there near that fallen tree!"

As I looked, I saw someone move between two trees. It was a man in a red jacket. I heard a shot, and a patch of snow exploded in front of me.

"Quick! Let's go over there!" I said. We ran off the trail, down the side of the mountain, and into a stand of trees. A bullet zinged above me, and another sank into the tree right next to Sam.

A man with a blond beard was looking out from behind a snowbank. I fired at him.

"*Auuugh!*" the man cried out.

I said, "Let's hurry up and get back to the sled! Down here!" We ran through the trees below the trail.

Suddenly a voice yelled, "Ellen!"

We stopped behind a snowbank and listened. Beside me, I could hear Sam breathing hard.

"Ellen!" the voice called again. "We know you're there!"

I shook my head. "What does he mean, 'Ellen'?" I asked.

Another voice called out, "Ellen! Give us the gold and we won't hurt you!"

"You're crazy!" I yelled. "There's no Ellen here!"

A shot rang out, and the top of the snowbank was blown off. We ran.

The sled was stopped in the middle of the trail. The dogs were lying down, resting.

Quint and Sonny were out of sight.

"Sonny!" I called softly. I knew he wouldn't be far from the gold.

"Over here!" Sonny said. His voice came from behind a large rock. Sam and I ran toward it. Suddenly I felt that someone was behind me. I turned to look. Two other men were there—right behind us!

I pushed Sam sideways. A shot just missed my arm. I raised my rifle and fired, and one of the men fell face down in the snow. The other man stopped. "Harry!" he said, as he bent over the fallen man.

I saw Sonny poking his head up from behind the rock. I called to him, "This way!" Quint and Sonny came out from behind the rock. Sonny's face was set in a hard, angry expression. We all ran up the side of the mountain to the sled.

Quint cracked the whip, and the dogs jumped forward. In the distance, the man in the red jacket fired. I knew he was too far away to hit us.

We raced to the top of the pass. We had to make it! After that we'd be going downhill, and it would be easy to leave the men far behind.

The climb was steep. The dogs panted and pulled. We grabbed their traces and pulled, too.

At last, we reached the top. "We made it!" I said. We started down. The snow got softer and deeper. It was up to my knees, then up to my waist. The dogs looked as if they were swimming. We slowed down, and soon we could hardly move.

Sonny made his way to the edge of the trail. "Down here!" he said. "The snow's not deep at all!"

Quint took a look. "Too steep," he said. "The sled would tip."

I could hear Sam saying softly, "Oh, no."

Two dogs started barking and growling. Quint went to see what was wrong. "Ruby and Zeke," he said. "Their traces are all mixed up!" I went to help. With every step I sank deep in the snow.

Quint and I unfastened Zeke's traces. Then I lifted him free. Suddenly Sam's rifle went off. "Look out!" he yelled. From above us, I heard another shot. Zeke's body jerked. He sank into the snow, dead.

I looked around. The man in the red jacket and the blond man were standing above us. A third man, tall and thin, was coming up from below. It was the man I'd seen bending over the one I had shot.

"Put your rifles down," said the man in the red jacket. We did. Sam put his down very slowly. He looked sick.

The three men came up to us, pointing their rifles. "Stand over there," the man in the red jacket said to us. We moved to the side of the trail.

The man in the red jacket walked up to Sam. "All right, Ellen. I want that gold."

"That's Sam," I said.

"Sam!" The man laughed. "She's fooled you! She's a liar all right! You think you have a boy here? Take a look!"

He jerked off Sam's green wool cap. I could hardly believe what I saw. Long, beautiful hair rolled out from that cap. It was red, and bright as a new penny. Sam was a woman!

She gave him a look of pure hate. "The gold's gone," she said. "I fell into Sawtooth Lake and lost it."

The tall man spoke up. "She's given it to them," he said. "Look in the sled, Bill."

"OK, keep them covered," said the man with the blond beard.

Bill had a rag around his bloody hand. He held it in front of my face. "You shot me and you killed Harry, too. You're going to die for this," he said.

Bill took the moosehide cover off the sled. I looked over at Sonny. His face was dark red. Bill took the gold pans and threw them out on the snow. Then he lifted out one of the bags of gold.

Sonny let out a roar! His face was wild. He charged after Bill. The man looked scared. He fired at Sonny, hitting him. Sonny grabbed his shoulder.

The tall man fired his rifle. I thought he hit Ellen, but she didn't fall. Then Quint's hand moved like lightning. His knife flew. It sank in the man's chest.

As the tall man fell, I grabbed his rifle. The man with the red jacket was aiming at Sonny. Then he saw me. "Hey!" he said. I fired, and he fell over in the snow.

Another shot rang out. When I looked around, Bill was dead, too. Quint had picked up a rifle and killed him with one shot.

All at once, the woods were quiet. I stared at the three dead men. Then I stared at her, at Ellen.

7

> The Truth
Comes Out

She stared back. She looked scared and angry. "Are you all right?" I said. I thought she had been hit.

"I'm OK, but Sonny's hurt," she said.

Quint was bent over Sonny. He'd been hit in the shoulder.

"It's not too bad," said Quint. "There's no bullet in there."

I tore up one of Sonny's shirts. We started wrapping it around his shoulder. "Take it easy," he said.

I could tell it hurt him a lot. "You're really crazy," I said, "the way you went after that guy. I don't know why you aren't dead. You have no sense at all."

"Lucky for you, I had no sense," said Sonny. He was grinning.

We finished taking care of Sonny. He

leaned back against the sled and stared at Ellen. I kept looking at her, too. I guess I couldn't help it.

"Who are you?" asked Sonny.

She said, "Ellen, like they said."

"Who were those men?" I asked.

"My Pa's partners," she said. "They were good men at first, until we found gold. Then they wanted it all. They killed Pa. They would have killed me, too, but I got away. I took the gold, all of it. Now it's at the bottom of Sawtooth Lake."

"So that bear had nothing to do with your father's death?" I asked.

"No," she said. "I was just tracking him because I was hungry. Everything else I told you is true."

We all kept looking at her. Very quickly, she rolled up her hair and put her cap back on. She didn't look like a boy to me, though—not anymore.

"Are we going to leave for Nome right away?" she said.

I looked at Sonny. "We'd better rest here for a while," I said.

"Then I'm going to take a walk," she said. "I'll be back soon."

Quint asked, "What should we do with these dead men?"

Sonny said, "How about just leaving them in the snow?"

Quint said, "Want to see what's in their pockets first?"

"That's the best idea you've had yet!" said Sonny.

Sonny watched Quint go through the dead men's pockets. I watched Ellen walking away through the snow.

"Hey," said Quint. "Rings!" He held up two wedding rings.

"Let's see," I said. The inside of one ring said, "From CWM to MAR, 6/11/77." The inside of the other said, "From MAR to CWM, 6/11/77."

"These might belong to Ellen," I said. I put them in my pocket and started to walk after her.

She was sitting on a log. She'd taken her cap off. I just stood there for a minute, looking at her. She turned and saw me. She got up, looking angry.

I held out the rings. "I thought these might be yours," I said.

She took the rings in her small hand.

"They *are* mine," she said slowly. "They were Mama's and Pa's . . . Cyrus Walker Macrae and Miriam Aimes Reddick." She covered her face with her hands and began to sob.

I tried to think of something to say. All I could think of was, "I'm sorry." I put my arm around her shoulders. I wanted to kiss her, but I had the sense not to try.

A few minutes later she stopped crying. She ducked away from my arm and stood up quickly. "Let's get back," she said. Her voice was hard, but her face looked so sad and tired. My heart seemed to twist in my chest.

Back by the sled, Quint and Sonny were half asleep. The dead men were out of sight.

Ellen walked up and said, "I need to say something to all of you."

Sonny sat up, smiling.

Ellen went on, "I was trying to look like a boy because . . . because it was easier. Now you know I'm not a boy. You'd better act like gentlemen around me. All of you." She gave Sonny a hard look. "Or you'll end up like that grizzly," she added.

Sonny jumped up, which must have hurt his shoulder. Gently, he took one of her small hands between his big ones. "Miss Ellen," he said, "I want to apologize. I know what you're thinking about. You didn't like the way I was talking the other night. No nice woman would. Well, I'm sorry as can be for sounding like such a fool. And I'm certainly going to act like a gentleman around you. That's a promise. Do you think you can forgive me?"

Ellen was surprised. "I guess so," she said.

"Thank you, Miss Ellen," said Sonny. He gave her a wide, warm smile. I remembered the women in San Francisco. I remembered how they would smile and stare when Sonny came into a room. I remembered Mary. It didn't make me feel good.

The next day we were out of food. I thought Sonny could stay and watch the sled. He had to rest his shoulder anyway. Quint, Ellen, and I could go off hunting.

Then Sonny said, "You don't need three people to hunt. Why don't you stay here, too, Miss Ellen? There's nothing for me to do but sit here. I'd just be thinking about my shoulder all day. I really would like it if you'd stay and talk to me."

"I'll stay," said Ellen. "I'm pretty tired. I wouldn't mind a rest, myself."

So Quint and I went off alone. I kept wondering what Ellen and Sonny were talking about.

We were headed down the side of the mountain. Quint walked toward the east side. I walked toward the west. The snow was better than on the trail, but it was still soft and deep. It was slow going.

We'd been hunting about an hour when Quint waved at me. I looked around. A deer was running my way. Quickly, I hid behind a tree. A moment later, I could hear the deer jumping through the soft snow. Just then, the deer went by. I aimed my rifle. I fired—and missed.

A minute later, Quint walked up. "You are no good today," he said. "You're thinking about *her,* not about food."

I stared at him. How could he know so much? "You're right," I said. I felt pretty low. Here I was, dreaming about Ellen, but I couldn't even catch her dinner.

8

Trouble with the Dogs

The next day we were on the move again. We went down the other side of the pass. It was hard work, and we were all hungry.

The snow was still soft. Quint and I broke the trail with snowshoes. Then Ellen followed with the sled. Sonny walked along with her. I could tell that his shoulder hurt, but he never said anything about it. Sonny was like that.

We stopped early so we could hunt. This time Ellen went, too. Our luck was poor, though. All we got were rabbits. Ellen and Quint got four each, and I got two. Each dog would have a small dinner, and the four of us would have nothing.

Back at camp, Quint started to cut up the rabbits for the dogs.

"Wait a minute!" said Sonny. "You're

going to cook those up for us."

"It's better for the dogs to eat," said Quint. "They need their strength."

"No, we come first," said Sonny. "The dogs can skip a couple of meals. It won't hurt them."

Quint looked at me. I knew the dogs should eat, but I was feeling too low to argue. I was hungry, too.

"Let's have the rabbit tonight, Quint," I said. "We'll have better luck tomorrow."

When the rabbit was cooked, Ellen took a lot for herself. She cut it up into several pieces. Then she took it out to the dogs!

Quint said, "That's one strong woman. She's stronger than most men!"

I thought about feeding my dinner to the dogs, too. They had worked harder that day than we had. But the meat was right in front of me, and it smelled so good. Quint was right. Ellen was one strong woman.

After we ate, Quint brought out the dogs' booties. Some of the booties had rips in them. "We need to fix these," he said.

"I'll help you," said Ellen. She took one of Quint's needles and went to work. She was quicker than Quint, and you could hardly see the rips when she was finished.

Ellen turned to Quint. "Tell me about some of your experiences on the trail," she said with a smile. "Didn't you say a moose charged your team once?"

Quint grinned. "Yes," he said.

"Want to tell me about it?" asked Ellen.

Quint looked at Sonny and me. He'd never told Ellen a story with Sonny and me right there.

"Go ahead," I said. "I'd like to hear it, too." Sonny went off to check the dogs' feet.

"OK," said Quint. "This was when I worked taking the mail. I used to take it from Fairbanks to Anchorage. I had a partner, Joe.

"One day we came up near Trapper Creek. I had the team, and Joe was walking in front. The snow was bad—almost like on Leggit Pass."

"I remember," said Ellen, with a frown.

Quint went on, "Then up ahead, I saw a moose. He was a big guy. His antlers were as wide as I am tall. Joe saw the moose, too. He yelled for me.

"I stopped the sled and looked for my gun. The gun wasn't there! It wasn't on the sled.

"The moose saw the dogs, and he came running at them. The dogs saw the moose, too. They were growling and barking. A big fight was coming if we didn't stop the moose. Maybe we'd lose some dogs.

"Joe fired and hit the moose here." Quint pointed to his ribs. "But that didn't stop him. I didn't know what to do. I had no gun. So I ran at the moose! I waved my arms. I yelled like crazy.

"The moose stopped. Then he turned around and ran away! I looked too crazy for the moose. We were lucky."

"Did you ever find your gun later?" Ellen asked.

"About a mile back. It had fallen off the sled," said Quint.

"Charging that moose was really brave," I said.

"Maybe it was crazy," said Quint.

"I'd like to hear more stories," I said.

"Anytime," said Quint.

I fell asleep thinking how lucky Joe had been to have Quint with him. Then I thought about how lucky Sonny and I were, too.

The next morning, Sonny brought his favorite dog, Teeka, up to Quint. "Let's make her lead dog today," he said. "I think she'll do better than Kip."

"You can't do that!" said Quint. "Kip has always been the lead dog."

"We'll try Teeka for a change. You put her in Kip's place." Sonny's voice had a hard edge to it.

I said, "Sonny, Quint knows dogs better than we do. Let's do what he says."

Sonny showed his teeth in an ugly grin. "Is that an order, Ben?"

That grin made me angry, but I didn't want a fight. "Quint knows what he's doing," I said.

Quint walked up to the dogs, who were resting in the snow. He took Kip and walked him up to his usual place in the lead. He said, "I'll do what Ben says. Ben has more sense." He looked at Sonny. "You have no more sense than a rabbit," he said. He started to fasten Kip into his traces.

Sonny marched up to Quint and grabbed his arm. "You're putting Teeka in there right now!" he said.

I ran up to Sonny. "Leave Quint alone!" I said.

Sonny turned. I saw that ugly grin again.

I couldn't stand it. I punched him in the jaw. Sonny fell back a little. Then he tried to grab my neck. Beside me, I saw Quint. His knife was in his hand.

Then a rifle went off with a boom. The three of us froze. Ellen was standing there, her rifle pointed at the sky. "That's enough. All of you," she said. Her voice was shaky.

We turned away from each other. We started getting the sled ready. No one said a word.

After a while I said to Ellen, "I'm sorry about that fight. I guess you're probably sick of us."

She said, "I'm sick of fighting—and killing."

"Nobody's going to get killed," I said.

She looked at me. That worried look was there. I wanted more than anything to see it disappear, to see her happy.

We were getting too hungry to travel. We stopped in the woods to hunt. We left Sonny behind with the sled. Again, all we got were rabbits, seven of them. We walked back to the sled feeling tired and hungry.

Even before we could see the sled, we heard the crack of the whip and loud barking. Then we saw the team. Sonny had put Teeka in the lead, and Kip was in Teeka's old place. He was growling and barking at Teeka.

"What does Sonny think he's doing?" I said.

"Sonny wants to be boss," said Quint.

Ellen looked at me. "Are you going to fight about this?" she said.

I thought a minute. "No," I said. "Quint, we'll try it. Let's just try it for today."

Quint said. "Kip knows he's the leader. I don't know what he'll do."

"See?" said Sonny, when we got up to the sled. "This is going to work out fine."

He was wrong. Kip wouldn't pull. He sat down in the snow and wouldn't move. With his good arm, Sonny used the whip. Kip cried out, but still he wouldn't pull.

"That's enough," I said. I let Kip loose from his traces. With a roar, he jumped at Teeka. Sonny hit him with the whip, but Kip didn't seem to feel it. Teeka grabbed his shoulder with her teeth. She tried to pull him down, but her traces held her. Kip's teeth were everywhere, snapping at Teeka. Then he got hold of her front leg. I rushed up and grabbed the back of his neck. There was a loud *crack*. Teeka's leg was broken. She sank down in the snow.

Sonny ran up, holding his rifle. "Get back," he yelled at Kip. He bent over Teeka and gently scratched her ears. He stood up, aiming the rifle with his good arm. "Hold still," he said softly, "that's a good girl." He pulled the trigger.

Then he raised his rifle and aimed it at Kip. "Now, you," he said.

I pointed my rifle at Sonny. "Put it down," I said. "We don't need two dogs dead."

He looked at me. His face was full of hate. Slowly, he put his rifle down. I put mine down, too. I could hardly believe I'd been pointing a gun at him. I said to myself, *Sonny used to be my friend.*

9

Lost in the Whiteness

The rest of the day, Sonny and I said very little to each other. I watched every move he made. I think he watched me just as carefully. Things were very strange between us now. Anything could happen.

All four of us were on edge. Being hungry made things worse. I thought about food for hours. Sometimes I swore I smelled bacon frying. I could almost see a big piece of bacon, right in front of me. I could almost taste it. Then I'd try hard to think about something—*anything*—else. I was driving myself crazy.

The dogs pulled slower and slower. Hunger made me so mean that I didn't even feel sorry for the dogs. I even thought about eating one of them.

It's funny, but when you're hungry gold

isn't worth much. I would have given all my gold for an apple.

Then, the next day, we finally had some luck. We were going along slowly though the woods in the late afternoon. Quint, who had the team, suddenly stopped the sled.

"Hear that?" he said.

We listened. We heard a roar, and then another.

"That's a moose—in trouble," said Quint.

We followed the sound. We cut though the woods. Before us was a wide meadow— and the moose. A pack of wolves was around him. They had cut the moose away from his herd. Now he was alone.

One wolf would run up to bite at the moose, then another, and another. They came from every direction. The moose would swing at them with his tall antlers, but the wolves kept coming.

"Stay with the sled!" Quint said to Sonny.

Ellen, Quint, and I ran out to the meadow. The wolves saw us and ran off. The moose took a step toward us. Then it turned and began to run away.

We stopped and aimed. Three rifle shots went off. They made my ears ring. The moose fell down on one knee, and then he got up. We fired again. The moose fell on its side and lay still.

Food! We ate and ate. When it grew dark, we built up the fire and ate again. We packed some of the meat for the rest of our trip. We felt wonderful. Sonny slapped Quint on the back as if they were old friends. I smiled at Sonny as if all that fighting had never happened.

We were sitting around the fire, talking. "Look!" said Ellen. Her voice was full of wonder. To the west, colors danced in the night sky: green, red, purple. It was the northern lights, the aurora borealis.

We watched. Nobody said anything for a long time. Then Sonny started singing quietly. It was a pretty song, a song for dancing. He got up and walked over to Ellen. He bent low and held out his hand. "May I have this dance?" he said.

She looked at him, surprised.

"Please, Miss Ellen," he said gently.

She smiled and got up. She put her hand carefully on his arm, below his hurt shoulder. He sang, and they started to dance together.

Round and round they went. The light from the fire danced on their faces. Behind them, waves of color danced in the sky.

I don't know how to dance. I never cared to until that moment. I watched Sonny and Ellen dancing. I felt so mean and small that I wished one of Sonny's legs had been hurt instead of his shoulder.

All the next day, he hung around her. That night he said to her, "I want to show you something."

He dug into our gear and got out the moosehide bags. "Just look at this," he said. He opened the bags. The gold flakes gleamed in the firelight.

"My," she said. She reached out slowly and picked up a little of the gold. She let it run through her fingers. It was like gold sand.

"I found it," said Sonny. "We had given up looking. Then I found a stream full of gold! You wouldn't believe how much! If only we'd stayed there. . . ."

"Maybe you can go back next spring," said Ellen.

"Maybe," said Sonny, "or maybe just go back to Frisco. This gold would buy a lot of good times, that's for sure."

"Or you could buy a house or some land," she said.

"That's what *I* want to buy," I said. "Land. I want to have a ranch someday."

She didn't say anything to that. After a minute or so, she said, "It's getting late. Guess I'll turn in."

Later that night I lay in my bearskin, thinking. I wondered what Ellen would do with a bag of gold. I thought about the ranch I wanted someday, and I kept seeing Ellen there with me. I had no idea if she'd want what I wanted, or if she'd ever want to be with me.

The next day it was snowing hard. Sonny, Quint, and Ellen were walking a little way ahead. I was behind with the team. After a while, Sonny dropped back to walk with me. The snow was blowing sideways, right in our faces, and we could hardly see.

Then Sonny said, "Hey, is something wrong with Ruby's left front paw?"

"Let's see," I said. We stopped to look, but we couldn't find anything.

"I guess she's OK," said Sonny. "I thought

I saw her having trouble with that foot."

The snow was falling harder. "I can't see the others," I said. "We should have yelled at them."

"Do you think they went this way?" Sonny pointed to the right.

"I'm not sure," I said.

"Want to run on ahead and look?" said Sonny. "I'll wait here."

"OK," I said. I started running. I could hardly see six feet in front of me. "Quint! Ellen!" I yelled.

I ran a little farther. I didn't see anyone. The snow blew against my face. I thought I'd better get back to Sonny before I got lost.

"Sonny!" I called. I ran back to where I'd left him and the sled. I found nothing but empty white space.

10

 Rescued by Quint

There were no tracks to follow. The falling snow had covered them. "Sonny!" I yelled. "Sonny! Quint! Ellen!" I ran the way I thought they had gone, yelling until my voice was hoarse. When I wasn't yelling, all I heard was silence.

I knew I must be going the wrong way. I would have run into them by now. I tried to go back the same way I'd come, but I wasn't sure which way that was.

I stopped running and sat down in the snow. I was lost. The snow fell without a sound. Already, it had covered my boots. I had an awful thought: the snow was going to bury me here.

I got up and started walking, but then I stopped. It was crazy to go farther. I had no idea where I was going. Also, the sun was going down and it was getting dark.

I wondered about Quint and Ellen and Sonny. I wondered if Sonny had tried to lose me. That seemed like a good bet. I wondered if Ellen was sorry I was gone. Without me, there would be less fighting, that was for sure. If she liked Sonny better, I was out of the way. I thought about Quint. Quint was probably sorry I was gone. I don't think he liked me much, but he liked me better than he liked Sonny.

Thinking about the others didn't give me much hope. I was sure that Quint would miss me, but he was the only person that I was sure of.

I lay down and let the snow cover me. I was too tired to care. Soon I fell asleep.

When I woke up, the snow had completely covered me. I hardly felt cold at all. I dug a small hole in front of my face for air. Then I fell asleep again.

When I woke up the second time, I knew it was morning. I punched my way out of the snow. There must have been more than a foot of snow on top of me. The morning was deep gray. It had stopped snowing, which gave me hope.

The snow was deep and soft. I would have given anything for snowshoes. I tried to get back to the place where I'd left Sonny, but I couldn't find it. Then I saw the sun. It was coming up behind me. It should have been coming up in front of me. Since I'd left Sonny, I had been walking the wrong way all that time!

I had no idea how far I was from the sled. I tried not to get scared. All I had were my clothes, my rifle, and three bullets. I had no matches. I had no blanket for when it got colder. I had no food. I had no idea how to get to Nome.

I wasn't sure how long I could last out here on my own.

I turned around and walked. I thought I found the place where I'd left Sonny, but I wasn't quite sure. I walked along what I thought was the trail. I wasn't sure of that, either.

I walked all day. I was hungry and tired. Often, I yelled, but I heard nothing. The only sound was my feet, walking in the snow. I'd never felt so alone.

"Keep going," I told myself. "Keep going. It's the only chance you've got."

As it started getting dark, I thought of spending another night alone in the snow. It gave me a cold feeling at the bottom of my stomach. "Help!" I yelled. "Help! HELP!"

Then, from very far away, I heard a voice! "Ben!"

"I'M HERE!" I yelled as loud as I could.

I ran toward the voice. I kept calling. I yelled, for now I knew who it was. I forgot that I was hungry and tired. I ran like a crazy man.

Quint's voice got louder, nearer. Then I saw him through the trees. I ran up to him and grabbed him by the shoulders. "Quint!" I said.

He even grinned. "I thought you were lost for good," he said.

"Me, too!" I said. "Boy, am I glad to see you!"

He said, "Ellen and I looked for you. We tried to find you all day." He frowned. "Sonny didn't want to. He said his shoulder hurt too much. He wanted to go on." Quint looked hard at me. "Sonny got you lost yesterday. I know."

"Yes," I said. "I know, too."

Quint showed me to the sled. It was

beginning to get dark. "Up here," said Quint. We climbed a small hill. Near the top, he turned to me. "Quiet," he said. "Sonny and Ellen are down there. Don't let them hear us."

"Why not?" I asked.

"Shhh!" Quint said. He went slowly to the top of the hill. He waved for me to follow.

I went behind him to the top. Down below was Ellen! My heart seemed to jump inside my chest. Across the fire was Sonny. His blond head was bent as he stirred the fire. His voice floated up to me. ". . . Best food in Frisco," he was saying. "Always full of people. Everyone dressed up fancy. I'll take you there sometime."

Quint's voice was low in my ear. "You shoot Sonny. Now."

I turned and looked at Quint.

"Now," said Quint. "Before he tries to kill you again."

11

Sonny Shows
a Dark Side

I thought of Sonny standing on the frozen lake, saying that the matches were lost. I thought of being lost yesterday. I thought of him dancing with Ellen, round and round, by the fire.

I shook my head. "I can't," I said. I could kill a man if I *had* to, I thought, but not like this.

"Then all I can say is that you'd better watch out," said Quint.

"I will," I said.

Quint and I walked down the hill. "Ben!" said Ellen when she saw us. I wondered how glad she was to see me. I wanted to see her face, but her back was to the fire.

Sonny slapped me on the back. "Glad to see you, pal!" he said. "I thought you were gone for good! How about some dinner?"

I ate. Sonny grinned at me across the fire. "I kept waiting for you yesterday," he said, "but you didn't show up. Then we heard you yelling. We followed your voice. We were yelling like crazy, but you kept getting farther and farther away. Finally we had to stop. It was snowing so hard we couldn't see a thing. How'd you spend the night?"

I told them.

"Smart idea," said Quint. "Not so cold under the snow."

Sonny said, "The next day we still couldn't find you. I thought maybe you'd fallen and got hurt, but then Quint finally found you. Good old Quint!"

"Good old Quint," I said. Sonny's face looked strange in the light of the fire. I looked away.

Sonny began humming that dance tune again. I felt the back of my neck turn red. Sonny walked over to Ellen. "May I have this dance, Miss Ellen?" he said.

Ellen shook her head. "No, thanks. I don't feel like dancing tonight," she said. She said it in a friendly way, though.

Sonny said, "Shucks, Miss Ellen. I'll just

find me another partner." He walked over to where the dogs were lying.

"Come here, Ruby," he called. He led Ruby over to the fire.

"Here we go, girl," he said. He picked up Ruby's front legs so that she was standing up. "One and a-two, and a-one and a-two," Sonny sang. He moved Ruby slowly around on her back legs. "That's a girl!" he said.

Ellen started laughing. It was a beautiful sound. I felt almost as lonely as I had last night. If I can't have Ellen, I thought, I might as well be lost.

The next morning, I woke up hot. It was warm, almost like summer. Quint felt the soft snow and frowned. "This will slow the dogs down," he said.

Before we ate, Ellen walked off by herself. I followed her. I wanted so much to see her alone.

She walked behind a stand of trees. As I watched, she rubbed her face with soft snow. Then she took a comb from her jacket. She began to comb her hair. How long it was! It went halfway down her back. It fell away from her comb in long red waves. My hands wanted to touch it. I walked a little closer and watched her from behind a bush.

She bent down to the snow. Very quickly, she stood up and threw a snowball at me.

I ducked, but it hit me hard on the forehead.

"Ellen!" I said. I stood up, rubbing my forehead.

"Stop sneaking up on me!" she said.

"I didn't mean to. I just wanted to see you," I said. I sounded stupid.

"Just stop sneaking up on me," she said. She rolled up her hair and pulled her cap over it. She walked back to the sled. Her feet were light and quick in the soft snow. I followed behind, feeling like a fool—a lonely fool.

After a quick breakfast, we started packing the sled.

"How close to Nome are we now?" asked Sonny.

"It's only about 75 miles farther," said Quint.

"Hey," said Sonny, "that's great!"

Ellen smiled at Quint. "Soon you can see your wife," she said.

"Wife!" I said. "You're married, Quint?"

Quint nodded. "Yes," he said.

Quint was married! He'd never told me or Sonny. Maybe if we'd been nicer to him, he would have. We didn't know anything about him at all.

"Any kids?" I asked Quint.

Quint grinned. "Two boys. They're big— almost as old as you."

That was another surprise. I had thought Quint was around 30, but he must have been more like 40.

We hit the trail. It led up a long, steep hill. Near the top, Quint waved at Sonny. "Stop the dogs!" he said. "Look over here!"

He led us through the trees. There, across the snowy woods, we saw blue—the dark blue water of Norton Sound. Nome was just up the coast!

Sonny threw back his head and let out a roar. "Here I come, Nome!" he yelled. "Better be ready!"

We ran back to the sled. The dogs felt our excitement. They ran quickly and eagerly over the snow.

Nome! Soon we'd be there! I wondered what Ellen's plans were. I was afraid to ask. I was afraid she wanted to stay with Sonny.

For weeks, I couldn't wait to get to Nome. Now I almost wanted to slow down. If this were to be the end of my days with Ellen, I wanted the time to last.

The day got warmer. The dogs' tongues hung out of their mouths. The trail led along the bottom of a high cliff. The snow was piled up high on the cliff above. Below the trail, a stream ran. The water was so bright from the sun that it hurt my eyes.

"Whoa!" called Sonny. He stopped the team. We walked back to him.

"Sled's not pulling right," he said. "I think something's caught under one of the runners."

Quint and I bent down to look, brushing the soft snow off the runners.

"Sonny!" said Ellen. Her voice sounded surprised and scared.

Quint and I looked up. Sonny was pointing his rifle at us. I stood up slowly. Somehow, I wasn't surprised.

12

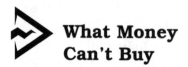

What Money Can't Buy

Sonny's blue eyes were bright and hard. *He hates me,* I thought. Now I knew this had been coming for a long time.

Sonny said in a loud voice, "This gold is mine, all of it! I'm the one who found it. And I worked harder than both of you to get it! You two wanted to quit. Quitters, both of you!"

He turned to Quint with a nasty grin. "I don't need a guide anymore, Quint. I can follow the coast right up to Nome." He pointed his rifle at my chest. "And you, Ben! I've never needed you. Never! You and Quint were against me from the start, but now I'm coming out on top! Ellen and I are going to Nome. You two are staying right here—until your bones rot!"

Ellen ran up to Sonny's side. "Don't kill

them!" she said. Her voice shook.

"I have to," said Sonny. He looked down his rifle barrel at my chest. "If I don't get them first, they'll—"

Ellen grabbed Sonny's hurt shoulder and pulled down hard. His mouth flew open in surprise and pain.

Sonny's rifle went off with a loud *boom!*

"No!" Quint screamed. I saw his knife flash by. Then the whole cliff above us seemed to fall.

A wall of white snow came rushing toward me. Before I could move a step, the wall hit me. White was everywhere. Then everything turned black.

When I opened my eyes, the white was still there. I felt as if I'd been punched all over. "I'm covered with snow," I thought. I pushed a hole in front of my face for air. Then I remembered everything: the shot from the rifle, Quint's scream, and then the avalanche. We must all be under the snow, I thought. Where was Ellen? I had to find her. I had to help her!

I began to dig my way forward. It was like swimming in powder. I didn't know where I was going. There was no up or down, only white snow in every direction. I wanted to scream. I would have done anything to see the sky.

I kept moving for I don't know how long. Then, at last, I felt something hard. A tree! I had touched the trunk of a tree.

I pushed my way along the side of the tree. Soon I felt branches. I was going up. Up! It seemed like hours. Then my hand broke through the snow. I shoved my face out and saw the sky! I took great mouthfuls of the cool, free air.

Above me, I heard the dogs, barking and crying. I started through the snow toward them.

About ten feet to my left, the snow moved, and Quint's face broke through.

"Quint!" I called.

He turned to me. "You're alive!" he said, a wide grin on his face.

"I hear the dogs," I said.

Quint listened. "And Ellen!" he said.

He was right! "Help!" she called. Her voice seemed very far away.

"ELLEN!" I yelled as loud as I could. "Ellen! We're coming!"

We climbed up the hill of snow. We

followed her voice. When we thought we were above her, we started digging. Soon we were panting like dogs.

"Up here!" we called. Her voice seemed to stay in the same place.

"She must be caught," said Quint.

We dug deep, deep in the snow. Then I saw the sleeve of her jacket! I pushed the snow away. Her hand reached out. I grabbed it and she held me.

We dug like crazy. At last, Ellen's face shook through the snow. "My leg's caught under the sled," she said.

We tried to pull her out, but that hurt her. We dug down toward the sled. Soon I heard water. The sled must have fallen near the stream, I thought.

At last we were able to lift the sled off her leg. "Is your leg OK?" I asked.

"I think so," she said. Her face was very pale. "You'd better look for the dogs—and Sonny."

"Let's get the shovel out," I said. Part of the sled was lying in the stream, and some of the gear had fallen out. The shovel was lying underwater.

Quint and I started digging for Sonny.

Soon Ellen joined in. "My leg's all right," she told me. "Nothing's broken."

After a while, Quint stood up and said, "Sonny is down here." I looked at Quint.

"He's dead," Quint said. I heard Ellen draw in her breath sharply.

I said, "Did the avalanche—?" Quint shook his head. "My knife got him first." He added, "Don't look."

I didn't want to. I wanted to remember the happy, funny friend Sonny used to be, before he found the gold.

We dug out the dogs. Boo and Ruby were dead. The rest had been lucky.

We rested a while, and then started on the sled. Most of the gear had fallen into the stream and been carried away by the water. We didn't see the bags of gold.

Then Quint said, "Look!" There, at the bottom of the stream, were a few flakes of gold. That was all. The rest of it was gone.

I sank down in the snow. I felt more tired than I'd ever been. My dream of a ranch seemed very, very far away. I said, "We can't even buy ourselves dinner in Nome."

"Yes, we can," said Ellen. Quint and I stared at her.

"I have gold," she said. She took off her jacket. She turned it inside out and handed it to me. "It's in here," she said. "I sewed it inside."

The jacket was heavy. I felt around the sleeves, around the edges, and around the collar. I could feel the hard-packed gold under the cloth.

She laughed a little. "That gold even saved my life," she said. "One of Pa's partners shot me. The bullet just hit my jacket and got stuck in the gold. It's still in there."

"So that's what happened," I said. "I *thought* I'd seen you get hit!"

She smiled. "I was afraid the gold would start spilling out, but it didn't," she said. "Anyway, it's your gold now, too. I want to share it with both of you."

"Thanks, lady," said Quint. "You have a good heart."

"Thank you," I said. I couldn't think of anything else to say, but I felt pretty good. Ellen had kept her gold a secret from Sonny, but not from Quint and me. Maybe she hadn't liked Sonny so much after all. It gave me a lot of hope.

By the time we got the sled back together, it was late. We were too tired to go far, but we didn't want to look at that huge pile of snow anymore—or think about what was buried there. After traveling a few miles, we stopped and built a fire.

I stared into the flames. I thought about how wrong you can be about people. I'd always thought Sonny was such a great guy, but the gold showed a part of him that was rotten. As for Quint, I hadn't liked him at all, but he turned out to be the one I could count on. And Ellen! At first, I'd thought she was a boy! Now that I knew her, I wanted her with me always, if she'd have me.

She was sitting next to me now. "Ellen?" I said. I held out my hand to her, and she took it.

After a while, the northern lights began to dance in the night sky. I felt as if Ellen and I were up there, dancing with them.